SELECTED POEMS
OF
# Emily
# Dickinson

SELECTED POEMS
OF
Emily
Dickinson

FALL RIVER PRESS

New York

# FALL RIVER PRESS

New York

An Imprint of Sterling Publishing
387 Park Avenue South
New York, NY 10016

Poem numbers in this selected edition are for purposes of reference and continuity.
They do not correspond to the assigned poem numbers
in standard editions of Emily Dickinson's complete poems.

This 2011 edition published by Fall River Press.

Cover art: St James's wallpaper/The Bridgeman Art Library International
Cover design by Scott Russo

ISBN 978-0-7607-9322-0

Manufactured in China

2  4  6  8  10  9  7  5  3

www.sterlingpublishing.com

# From the Introduction to
## *The Collected Poems of Emily Dickinson*

$\mathcal{M}$ANY of [Emily Dickinson's] poems have been reprinted in anthologies, selections, textbooks for recitation, and they have increasingly found their elect and been best interpreted by the expansion of those lives they have seized upon by force of their natural, profound intuition of the miracles of everyday Life, Love, and Death.

She herself was of the part of life that is always youth, always magical. She wrote of it as she grew to know it, step by step, discovery by discovery, truth by truth — until time merely became eternity. She was preëminently the discoverer — eagerly hunting the meaning of it all; this strange world in which she wonderingly found herself, — "A Balboa of house and garden," surmising what lay beyond the purple horizon.

She lived with a God we do not believe in, and trusted in an immortality we do not deserve, in that confiding age when Duty ruled over Pleasure before the Puritan became a hypocrite.

Her aspect of Deity, — as her intimation, — was her own, — unique, peculiar, unimpaired by the brimstone theology of her day.

Her poems reflect this direct relation toward the great realities we have later avoided, covered up, or tried to wipe out; perhaps because were they really so great we become so small in consequence. All truth came to Emily straight from honor to honor unimpaired. She never trafficked with falsehood seriously, never employed a deception in thought or feeling of her own. This pitiless sincerity dictated:

> "I like a look of agony
> Because I know it's true
> Men do not sham convulsion
> Nor simulate a throe."

As light after darkness, Summer following Winter, she is inevitable, unequivocal. Evasion of fact she knew not, though her body might flit away from interruption, leaving an intruder to "Think that a sunbeam left the door ajar."

Her entities were vast — as her words were few; those words like dry-point etching or frost upon the pane! Doubly aspected, every event, every object seemed to hold for her both its actual and imaginative dimension. By this power she carries her readers behind the veil obscuring less gifted apprehension. She even descends over the brink of the grave to toy with the outworn vesture of the spirit, recapture the dead smile on lips surrendered forever; then, as on the wings of Death, betakes herself and her reader in the direction of the escaping soul to new, incredible heights.

Doubly her life carried on, two worlds in her brown eyes, by which habit of the Unseen she confessed:

"I fit for them,
I seek the dark till I am thorough fit.
The labor is a solemn one,
With this sufficient sweet —
That abstinence as mine produce
A purer good for them,
If I succeed, —
If not, I had
The transport of the Aim."

This transport of the aim absorbed her, and this absorption is her clearest explanation, — the absorption in This excluding observance of That. Most of all she was busy. It takes time even for genius to crystallize the thought with which her letters and poems are crammed. Her solitude was never idle.

Her awe of that unknown sacrament of love permeated all she wrote, and before Nature, God, and Death she is more fearless than that archangel of portentous shadow she instinctively dreaded.

Almost transfigured by reverence, her poems are pervaded by inference sharply in contrast to the balder speech of to-day. Here the mystic suppressed the woman, though her heart leaped up over children, — radiant phenomena to her, akin to stars fallen among her daffodils in the orchard; and her own renunciation, chalice at lip, was nobly, frankly given in the poem ending:

"Each bound the other's crucifix,
We gave no other bond.
Sufficient troth that we shall rise —
Deposed, at length, the grave —
To that new marriage, justified
Through Calvaries of Love!"

Her own philosophy had early taught her that All was in All: there were no degrees in anything. Accordingly nothing was mean or trivial, and her "fainting robin" became a synonym of the universe. She saw in absolute terms which gave her poetry an accuracy like that obtained under the microscope of modern science. But her soul dominated, and when her footsteps wavered her terms were still dictated by her unquenchable spirit.

Hers too were spirit terms with life and friends, in which respect she was of a divergence from the usual not easily to be condoned.

It was precisely the clamor of the commonplace exasperated by the austerities of a reserved individuality, that provoked her immortal exclamation:

"Much madness is divinest sense
To a discerning eye.
Much sense the starkest madness;
'Tis the majority
In this, as all prevails.
Assent and you are sane —
Demur — you're straightway dangerous
And handled with a chain."

Her interpretation demands height and depth of application in her readers, for although her range is that of any soul not earth-bound by the senses, she does not always make it immediately plain when she speaks out of her own vision in her own tongue. In spite of which, beyond those who profess her almost as a cult, she is supremely the poet of those who "never read poetry." The scoffers, the literary agnostics, make exception for her. She is also the poet of the unpoetic, the unlearned foreigner, the busy, practical, inexpressive man as well as woman, the wise young and groping old, the nature worshipper, the schoolgirl, children caught by her fairy lineage, and lovers of all degree.

Full many a preacher has found her line at the heart of his matter and left her verse to fly up with his conclusion. And it is the Very Reverend head of a most Catholic order who writes, "I bless God for Emily, — some of her writings have had a more profound influence on my life than anything else that any one has ever written."

Mystic to mystic, mind to mind, spirit to spirit, dust to dust. She was at the source of things and dwelt beside the very springs of life, yet those deep wells from which she drew were of the wayside, though their waters were of eternal truth, her magnificat one of the certainties of every immortal being. Here in her poems the arisen Emily, unabashed by mortal bonds, speaks to her "Divine Majority":

> "Split the lark and you'll find the music —
> Bulb after bulb, in silver rolled,
> Scantily dealt to the Summer morning,
> Saved for your ears when lutes are old."

But in what vernacular explain the skylark to the mole — even she was at loss to tell. And for the true lovers of the prose or poetry of Emily Dickinson, explanation of her is as impertinent as unnecessary.

Martha Dickinson Bianchi.

# PART ONE

## Life

*This is my letter to the world,*
*  That never wrote to me, —*
*The simple news that Nature told,*
*  With tender majesty.*

*Her message is committed*
*  To hands I cannot see;*
*For love of her, sweet countrymen,*
*  Judge tenderly of me!*

## I

Success is counted sweetest
By those who ne'er succeed.
To comprehend a nectar
Requires sorest need.

Not one of all the purple host
Who took the flag to-day
Can tell the definition,
So clear, of victory,

As he, defeated, dying,
On whose forbidden ear
The distant strains of triumph
Break, agonized and clear.

## II

$O$UR share of night to bear,
Our share of morning,
Our blank in bliss to fill,
Our blank in scorning.

Here a star, and there a star,
Some lose their way.
Here a mist, and there a mist,
Afterwards — day!

## III

$I$F I can stop one heart from breaking,
I shall not live in vain;
If I can ease one life the aching,
Or cool one pain,
Or help one fainting robin
Unto his nest again,
I shall not live in vain.

## IV

A wounded deer leaps highest,
  I've heard the hunter tell;
'Tis but the ecstasy of death,
And then the brake is still.

The smitten rock that gushes,
The trampled steel that springs:
A cheek is always redder
Just where the hectic stings!

Mirth is the mail of anguish,
In which it caution arm,
Lest anybody spy the blood
And "You're hurt" exclaim!

## V

*C*HE heart asks pleasure first,
And then, excuse from pain;
And then, those little anodynes
That deaden suffering;

And then, to go to sleep;
And then, if it should be
The will of its Inquisitor,
The liberty to die.

## VI

*M*UCH madness is divinest sense
To a discerning eye;
Much sense the starkest madness.
'Tis the majority
In this, as all, prevails.
Assent, and you are sane;
Demur, — you're straightway dangerous,
And handled with a chain.

## VII

THE soul selects her own society,
Then shuts the door;
On her divine majority
Obtrude no more.

Unmoved, she notes the chariot's pausing
At her low gate;
Unmoved, an emperor is kneeling
Upon her mat.

I've known her from an ample nation
Choose one;
Then close the valves of her attention
Like stone.

## VIII

$\mathcal{P}$AIN has an element of blank;
It cannot recollect
When it began, or if there were
A day when it was not.

It has no future but itself,
Its infinite realms contain
Its past, enlightened to perceive
New periods of pain.

## IX

$\mathcal{I}$ TASTE a liquor never brewed,
From tankards scooped in pearl;
Not all the vats upon the Rhine
Yield such an alcohol!

Inebriate of air am I,
And debauchee of dew,
Reeling, through endless summer days,
From inns of molten blue.

When landlords turn the drunken bee
Out of the foxglove's door,
When butterflies renounce their drams,
I shall but drink the more!

Till seraphs swing their snowy hats,
And saints to windows run,
To see the little tippler
Leaning against the sun!

## X

*I* HAD no time to hate, because
The grave would hinder me,
And life was not so ample I
Could finish enmity.

Nor had I time to love; but since
Some industry must be,
The little toil of love, I thought,
Was large enough for me.

## XI

THE brain within its groove
Runs evenly and true;
But let a splinter swerve,
'Twere easier for you
To put the water back
When floods have slit the hills,
And scooped a turnpike for themselves,
And blotted out the mills!

## XII

I'M nobody! Who are you?
Are you nobody, too?
Then there's a pair of us — don't tell!
They'd banish us, you know.

How dreary to be somebody!
How public, like a frog
To tell your name the livelong day
To an admiring bog!

## XIII

THE nearest dream recedes, unrealized.
    The heaven we chase
    Like the June bee
    Before the school-boy
    Invites the race;
    Stoops to an easy clover —
Dips — evades — teases — deploys;
    Then to the royal clouds
    Lifts his light pinnace
    Heedless of the boy
Staring, bewildered, at the mocking sky.

    Homesick for steadfast honey,
    Ah! the bee flies not
That brews that rare variety.

## XIV

$W$E play at paste,
Till qualified for pearl,
Then drop the paste,
And deem ourself a fool.
The shapes, though, were similar,
And our new hands
Learned gem-tactics
Practising sands.

## XV

$I$ FOUND the phrase to every thought
I ever had, but one;
And that defies me, — as a hand
Did try to chalk the sun

To races nurtured in the dark; —
How would your own begin?
Can blaze be done in cochineal,
Or noon in mazarin?

## XVI

Hope is the thing with feathers
That perches in the soul,
And sings the tune without the words,
And never stops at all,

And sweetest in the gale is heard;
And sore must be the storm
That could abash the little bird
That kept so many warm.

I've heard it in the chillest land,
And on the strangest sea;
Yet, never, in extremity,
It asked a crumb of me.

## XVII

*D*ARE you see a soul at the white heat?
  Then crouch within the door.
Red is the fire's common tint;
  But when the vivid ore

Has sated flame's conditions,
  Its quivering substance plays
Without a color but the light
  Of unanointed blaze.

Least village boasts its blacksmith,
  Whose anvil's even din
Stands symbol for the finer forge
  That soundless tugs within,

Refining these impatient ores
  With hammer and with blaze,
Until the designated light
  Repudiate the forge.

## XVIII

*I* CAN wade grief,
Whole pools of it, —
I'm used to that.
But the least push of joy
Breaks up my feet,
And I tip — drunken.
Let no pebble smile,
'Twas the new liquor, —
That was all!

Power is only pain,
Stranded, through discipline,
Till weights will hang.
Give balm to giants,
And they'll wilt, like men.
Give Himmaleh, —
They'll carry him!

## XIX

*I* NEVER hear the word "escape"
Without a quicker blood,
A sudden expectation,
A flying attitude.

I never hear of prisons broad
By soldiers battered down,
But I tug childish at my bars, —
Only to fail again!

## XX

*F*OR each ecstatic instant
We must an anguish pay
In keen and quivering ratio
To the ecstasy.

For each beloved hour
Sharp pittances of years,
Bitter contested farthings
And coffers heaped with tears.

## XXI

THE thought beneath so slight a film
Is more distinctly seen, —
As laces just reveal the surge,
Or mists the Apennine.

## XXII

SURGEONS must be very careful
When they take the knife!
Underneath their fine incisions
Stirs the culprit, — Life!

## XXIII

I LIKE to see it lap the miles,
And lick the valleys up,
And stop to feed itself at tanks;
And then, prodigious, step

Around a pile of mountains,
And, supercilious, peer
In shanties by the sides of roads;
And then a quarry pare

To fit its sides, and crawl between,
Complaining all the while
In horrid, hooting stanza;
Then chase itself down hill

And neigh like Boanerges;
Then, punctual as a star,
Stop — docile and omnipotent —
At its own stable door.

### XXIV

THE show is not the show,
But they that go.
Menagerie to me
My neighbor be.
Fair play —
Both went to see.

## XXV

DELIGHT becomes pictorial
When viewed through pain, —
More fair, because impossible
That any gain.

The mountain at a given distance
In amber lies;
Approached, the amber flits a little, —
And that's the skies!

## XXVI

A THOUGHT went up my mind to-day
That I have had before,
But did not finish, — some way back,
I could not fix the year,

Nor where it went, nor why it came
The second time to me,
Nor definitely what it was,
Have I the art to say.

But somewhere in my soul, I know
I've met the thing before;
It just reminded me — 'twas all —
And came my way no more.

## XXVII

THOUGH I get home how late, how late!
So I get home, 'twill compensate.
Better will be the ecstasy
That they have done expecting me,
When, night descending, dumb and dark,
They hear my unexpected knock.
Transporting must the moment be,
Brewed from decades of agony!

To think just how the fire will burn,
Just how long-cheated eyes will turn
To wonder what myself will say,
And what itself will say to me,
Beguiles the centuries of way!

## XXVIII

*V*ICTORY comes late,
And is held low to freezing lips
Too rapt with frost
To take it.
How sweet it would have tasted,
Just a drop!
Was God so economical?
His table's spread too high for us
Unless we dine on tip-toe.
Crumbs fit such little mouths,
Cherries suit robins;
The eagle's golden breakfast
Strangles them.
God keeps his oath to sparrows,
Who of little love
Know how to starve!

## XXIX

*F*AITH is a fine invention
For gentlemen who see;
But microscopes are prudent
In an emergency!

## XXX

*A* SHADY friend for torrid days
Is easier to find
Than one of higher temperature
For frigid hour of mind.

The vane a little to the east
Scares muslin souls away;
If broadcloth breasts are firmer
Than those of organdy,

Who is to blame? The weaver?
Ah! the bewildering thread!
The tapestries of paradise
So notelessly are made!

## XXXI

$\mathcal{E}$ACH life converges to some centre
Expressed or still;
Exists in every human nature
A goal,

Admitted scarcely to itself, it may be,
Too fair
For credibility's temerity
To dare.

Adored with caution, as a brittle heaven,
To reach
Were hopeless as the rainbow's raiment
To touch,

Yet persevered toward, surer for the distance;
How high
Unto the saints' slow diligence
The sky!

Ungained, it may be, by a life's low venture,
But then,
Eternity enables the endeavoring
Again.

## XXXII

BEFORE I got my eye put out,
I liked as well to see
As other creatures that have eyes,
And know no other way.

But were it told to me, to-day,
That I might have the sky
For mine, I tell you that my heart
Would split, for size of me.

The meadows mine, the mountains mine, —
All forests, stintless stars,
As much of noon as I could take
Between my finite eyes.

The motions of the dipping birds,
The lightning's jointed road,
For mine to look at when I liked, —
The news would strike me dead!

So, safer, guess, with just my soul
Upon the window-pane
Where other creatures put their eyes,
Incautious of the sun.

## XXXIII

HE preached upon "breadth" till it argued him
  narrow, —
The broad are too broad to define;
And of "truth" until it proclaimed him a liar, —
The truth never flaunted a sign.

Simplicity fled from his counterfeit presence
As gold the pyrites would shun.
What confusion would cover the innocent Jesus
To meet so enabled a man!

## XXXIV

$G$OOD night! which put the candle out?
  A jealous zephyr, not a doubt.
  Ah! friend, you little knew
How long at that celestial wick
The angels labored diligent;
  Extinguished, now, for you!

It might have been the lighthouse spark
Some sailor, rowing in the dark,
  Had importuned to see!
It might have been the waning lamp
That lit the drummer from the camp
  To purer reveille!

## XXXV

$I$ HAD been hungry all the years;
  My noon had come, to dine;
  I, trembling, drew the table near,
  And touched the curious wine.

'Twas this on tables I had seen,
When turning, hungry, lone,
I looked in windows, for the wealth
I could not hope to own.

I did not know the ample bread,
'Twas so unlike the crumb
The birds and I had often shared
In Nature's dining-room.

The plenty hurt me, 'twas so new, —
Myself felt ill and odd,
As berry of a mountain bush
Transplanted to the road.

Nor was I hungry; so I found
That hunger was a way
Of persons outside windows,
The entering takes away.

## XXXVI

*I* YEARS had been from home,
And now, before the door,
I dared not open, lest a face
I never saw before

Stare vacant into mine
And ask my business there.
My business, — just a life I left,
Was such still dwelling there?

I fumbled at my nerve,
I scanned the windows near;
The silence like an ocean rolled,
And broke against my ear.

I laughed a wooden laugh
That I could fear a door,
Who danger and the dead had faced,
But never quaked before.

I fitted to the latch
My hand, with trembling care,
Lest back the awful door should spring,
And leave me standing there.

I moved my fingers off
As cautiously as glass,
And held my ears, and like a thief
Fled gasping from the house.

## XXXVII

*I* KNOW that he exists
Somewhere, in silence.
He has hid his rare life
From our gross eyes.

'Tis an instant's play,
'Tis a fond ambush,
Just to make bliss
Earn her own surprise!

But should the play
Prove piercing earnest,
Should the glee glaze
In death's stiff stare,

Would not the fun
Look too expensive?
Would not the jest
Have crawled too far?

## XXXVIII

HOPE is a subtle glutton;
   He feeds upon the fair;
And yet, inspected closely,
   What abstinence is there!

His is the halcyon table
   That never seats but one,
And whatsoever is consumed
   The same amounts remain.

## XXXIX

HEAVEN is what I cannot reach!
The apple on the tree,
Provided it do hopeless hang,
That "heaven" is, to me.

The color on the cruising cloud,
The interdicted ground
Behind the hill, the house behind, —
There Paradise is found!

## XL

A WORD is dead
When it is said,
Some say.
I say it just
Begins to live
That day.

## XLI

DROWNING is not so pitiful
  As the attempt to rise.
Three times, 'tis said, a sinking man
  Comes up to face the skies,
And then declines forever
  To that abhorred abode

Where hope and he part company, —
  For he is grasped of God.
The Maker's cordial visage,
  However good to see,
Is shunned, we must admit it,
  Like an adversity.

## XLII

$\mathcal{I}$F the foolish call them "flowers",
   Need the wiser tell?
If the savants "classify" them,
   It is just as well!

Those who read the *Revelations*
   Must not criticise
Those who read the same edition
   With beclouded eyes!

Could we stand with that old Moses
   Canaan denied, —
Scan, like him, the stately landscape
   On the other side, —

Doubtless we should deem superfluous
   Many sciences
Not pursued by learnèd angels
   In scholastic skies!

Low amid that glad *Belles lettres*
Grant that we may stand,
Stars, amid profound Galaxies,
At that grand "Right hand"!

## XLIII

 COULD mortal lip divine
 The undeveloped freight
Of a delivered syllable,
 'Twould crumble with the weight.

## XLIV

 MY life closed twice before its close;
 It yet remains to see
If Immortality unveil
 A third event to me,

So huge, so hopeless to conceive,
 As these that twice befell.
Parting is all we know of heaven,
 And all we need of hell.

## XLV

WE never know how high we are
  Till we are called to rise;
And then, if we are true to plan,
  Our statures touch the skies.

The heroism we recite
  Would be a daily thing,
Did not ourselves the cubits warp
  For fear to be a king.

## XLVI

THERE is no frigate like a book
  To take us lands away,
Nor any coursers like a page
  Of prancing poetry.

This traverse may the poorest take
  Without oppress of toll;
How frugal is the chariot
  That bears a human soul!

## XLVII

*W*HO has not found the heaven below
　Will fail of it above.
God's residence is next to mine,
　His furniture is love.

## XLVIII

*A* FACE devoid of love or grace,
　A hateful, hard, successful face,
　A face with which a stone
Would feel as thoroughly at ease
As were they old acquaintances, —
　First time together thrown.

## XLIX

*I* FELT a cleavage in my mind
　As if my brain had split;
I tried to match it, seam by seam,
　But could not make them fit.

The thought behind I strove to join
  Unto the thought before,
But sequence ravelled out of reach
  Like balls upon a floor.

## L

*I*F recollecting were forgetting,
  Then I remember not;
And if forgetting, recollecting,
  How near I had forgot!
And if to miss were merry,
  And if to mourn were gay,
How very blithe the fingers
  That gathered these to-day!

## LI

*A*RE friends delight or pain?
Could bounty but remain
Riches were good.

But if they only stay
Bolder to fly away,
Riches are sad.

## LII

*A*SHES denote that fire was;
Respect the grayest pile
For the departed creature's sake
That hovered there awhile.

Fire exists the first in light,
And then consolidates, —
Only the chemist can disclose
Into what carbonates.

## LIII

*F*ATE slew him, but he did not drop;
　　She felled — he did not fall —
Impaled him on her fiercest stakes —
　　He neutralized them all.

She stung him, sapped his firm advance,
　　But, when her worst was done,
And he, unmoved, regarded her,
　　Acknowledged him a man.

## LIV

*F*INITE to fail, but infinite to venture.
　　For the one ship that struts the shore
Many's the gallant, overwhelmed creature
　　Nodding in navies nevermore.

## LV

$\mathcal{I}$ MEASURE every grief I meet
  With analytic eyes;
I wonder if it weighs like mine,
  Or has an easier size.

I wonder if they bore it long,
  Or did it just begin?
I could not tell the date of mine,
  It feels so old a pain.

I wonder if it hurts to live,
  And if they have to try,
And whether, could they choose between,
  They would not rather die.

I wonder if when years have piled —
  Some thousands — on the cause
Of early hurt, if such a lapse
  Could give them any pause;

Or would they go on aching still
  Through centuries above,

Enlightened to a larger pain
  By contrast with the love.

The grieved are many, I am told;
  The reason deeper lies, —
Death is but one and comes but once,
  And only nails the eyes.

There's grief of want, and grief of cold, —
  A sort they call "despair";
There's banishment from native eyes,
  In sight of native air.

And though I may not guess the kind
  Correctly, yet to me
A piercing comfort it affords
  In passing Calvary,

To note the fashions of the cross,
  Of those that stand alone,
Still fascinated to presume
  That some are like my own.

## LVI

$\mathcal{I}$T dropped so low in my regard
   I heard it hit the ground,
And go to pieces on the stones
   At bottom of my mind;

Yet blamed the fate that fractured, less
   Than I reviled myself
For entertaining plated wares
   Upon my silver shelf.

## LVII

$\mathcal{L}$IFE, and Death, and Giants
   Such as these, are still.
Minor apparatus, hopper of the mill,
Beetle at the candle,
   Or a fife's small fame,
Maintain by accident
   That they proclaim.

## LVIII

REMEMBRANCE has a rear and front, —
    'Tis something like a house;
It has a garret also
    For refuse and the mouse,

Besides, the deepest cellar
    That ever mason hewed;
Look to it, by its fathoms
    Ourselves be not pursued.

## LIX

To hang our head ostensibly,
    And subsequent to find
That such was not the posture
    Of our immortal mind,

Affords the sly presumption
    That, in so dense a fuzz,
You, too, take cobweb attitudes
    Upon a plane of gauze!

## LX

*T*HE brain is wider than the sky,
  For, put them side by side,
The one the other will include
  With ease, and you beside.

The brain is deeper than the sea,
  For, hold them, blue to blue,
The one the other will absorb,
  As sponges, buckets do.

The brain is just the weight of God,
  For, lift them, pound for pound,
And they will differ, if they do,
  As syllable from sound.

## LXI

*T*HE bone that has no marrow;
  What ultimate for that?
It is not fit for table,
  For beggar, or for cat.

A bone has obligations,
  A being has the same;
A marrowless assembly
  Is culpabler than shame.

But how shall finished creatures
  A function fresh obtain? —
Old Nicodemus' phantom
  Confronting us again!

## LXII

THE past is such a curious creature,
  To look her in the face
A transport may reward us,
  Or a disgrace.

Unarmed if any meet her,
  I charge him, fly!
Her rusty ammunition
  Might yet reply!

## LXIII

*W*HAT soft, cherubic creatures
   These gentlewomen are!
One would as soon assault a plush
   Or violate a star.

Such dimity convictions,
   A horror so refined
Of freckled human nature,
   Of Deity ashamed, —

It's such a common glory,
   A fisherman's degree!
Redemption, brittle lady,
   Be so, ashamed of thee.

## LXIV

*W*HO never wanted, — maddest joy
   Remains to him unknown;
The banquet of abstemiousness
   Surpasses that of wine.

Within its hope, though yet ungrasped
    Desire's perfect goal,
No nearer, lest reality
    Should disenthrall thy soul.

## LXV

IT might be easier
    To fail with land in sight,
Than gain my blue peninsula
    To perish of delight.

## LXVI

I STEPPED from plank to plank
    So slow and cautiously;
The stars about my head I felt,
    About my feet the sea.

I knew not but the next
    Would be my final inch, —
This gave me that precarious gait
    Some call experience.

## LXVII

SOFTENED by Time's consummate plush,
   How sleek the woe appears
That threatened childhood's citadel
   And undermined the years!

Bisected now by bleaker griefs,
   We envy the despair
That devastated childhood's realm,
   So easy to repair.

# PART TWO

# Nature

My nosegays are for captives;
Dim, long-expectant eyes,
Fingers denied the plucking,
Patient till paradise.

To such, if they should whisper
Of morning and the moor,
They bear no other errand,
And I, no other prayer.

# I

*N*ATURE, the gentlest mother,
Impatient of no child,
The feeblest or the waywardest, —
Her admonition mild

In forest and the hill
By traveller is heard,
Restraining rampant squirrel
Or too impetuous bird.

How fair her conversation,
A summer afternoon, —
Her household, her assembly;
And when the sun goes down

Her voice among the aisles
Incites the timid prayer
Of the minutest cricket,
The most unworthy flower.

When all the children sleep
She turns as long away
As will suffice to light her lamps;
Then, bending from the sky,

With infinite affection
And infiniter care,
Her golden finger on her lip,
Wills silence everywhere.

## II

*B*EFORE you thought of spring,
Except as a surmise,
You see, God bless his suddenness,
A fellow in the skies
Of independent hues,
A little weather-worn,
Inspiriting habiliments
Of indigo and brown.

With specimens of song,
As if for you to choose,
Discretion in the interval,
With gay delays he goes
To some superior tree
Without a single leaf,
And shouts for joy to nobody
But his seraphic self!

### III

ONE of the ones that Midas touched,
Who failed to touch us all,
Was that confiding prodigal,
The blissful oriole.

So drunk, he disavows it
With badinage divine;
So dazzling, we mistake him
For an alighting mine.

A pleader, a dissembler,
An epicure, a thief, —
Betimes an oratorio,
An ecstasy in chief;

The Jesuit of orchards,
He cheats as he enchants
Of an entire attar
For his decamping wants.

The splendor of a Burmah,
The meteor of birds,
Departing like a pageant
Of ballads and of bards.

I never thought that Jason sought
For any golden fleece;
But then I am a rural man,
With thoughts that make for peace.

But if there were a Jason,
Tradition suffer me
Behold his lost emolument
Upon the apple-tree.

## IV

*I* DREADED that first robin so,
But he is mastered now,
And I'm accustomed to him grown, —
He hurts a little, though.

I thought if I could only live
Till that first shout got by,
Not all pianos in the woods
Had power to mangle me.

I dared not meet the daffodils,
For fear their yellow gown
Would pierce me with a fashion
So foreign to my own.

I wished the grass would hurry,
So when 'twas time to see,
He'd be too tall, the tallest one
Could stretch to look at me.

I could not bear the bees should come,
I wished they'd stay away
In those dim countries where they go:
What word had they for me?

They're here, though; not a creature failed,
No blossom stayed away
In gentle deference to me,
The Queen of Calvary.

Each one salutes me as he goes,
And I my childish plumes
Lift, in bereaved acknowledgment
Of their unthinking drums.

## V

*A* ROUTE of evanescence
With a revolving wheel;
A resonance of emerald,
A rush of cochineal;
And every blossom on the bush
Adjusts its tumbled head, —
The mail from Tunis, probably,
An easy morning's ride.

## VI

*T*WO butterflies went out at noon
And waltzed above a stream,
Then stepped straight through the firmament
And rested on a beam;

And then together bore away
Upon a shining sea, —
Though never yet, in any port,
Their coming mentioned be.

If spoken by the distant bird,
If met in ether sea
By frigate or by merchantman,
Report was not to me.

## VII

*I* STARTED early, took my dog,
And visited the sea;
The mermaids in the basement
Came out to look at me,

And frigates in the upper floor
Extended hempen hands,
Presuming me to be a mouse
Aground, upon the sands.

But no man moved me till the tide
Went past my simple shoe,
And past my apron and my belt,
And past my bodice too,

And made as he would eat me up
As wholly as a dew
Upon a dandelion's sleeve —
And then I started too.

And he — he followed close behind;
I felt his silver heel
Upon my ankle, — then my shoes
Would overflow with pearl.

Until we met the solid town,
No man he seemed to know;
And bowing with a mighty look
At me, the sea withdrew.

## VIII

*A* BIRD came down the walk:
He did not know I saw;
He bit an angle-worm in halves
And ate the fellow, raw.

And then he drank a dew
From a convenient grass,
And then hopped sidewise to the wall
To let a beetle pass.

He glanced with rapid eyes
That hurried all abroad, —
They looked like frightened beads, I thought
He stirred his velvet head

Like one in danger; cautious,
I offered him a crumb,
And he unrolled his feathers
And rowed him softer home

Than oars divide the ocean,
Too silver for a seam,
Or butterflies, off banks of noon,
Leap, plashless, as they swim.

## IX

$\mathcal{A}$ NARROW fellow in the grass
Occasionally rides;
You may have met him, — did you not?
His notice sudden is.

The grass divides as with a comb,
A spotted shaft is seen;
And then it closes at your feet
And opens further on.

He likes a boggy acre,
A floor too cool for corn.
Yet when a child, and barefoot,
I more than once, at morn,

Have passed, I thought, a whip-lash
Unbraiding in the sun, —
When, stooping to secure it,
It wrinkled, and was gone.

Several of nature's people
I know, and they know me;
I feel for them a transport
Of cordiality;

But never met this fellow,
Attended or alone,
Without a tighter breathing,
And zero at the bone.

## X

THERE came a wind like a bugle;
It quivered through the grass,
And a green chill upon the heat
So ominous did pass
We barred the windows and the doors
As from an emerald ghost;
The doom's electric moccason
That very instant passed.
On a strange mob of panting trees,

And fences fled away,
And rivers where the houses ran
The living looked that day.
The bell within the steeple wild
The flying tidings whirled.
How much can come
And much can go,
And yet abide the world!

## XI

*A* SPIDER sewed at night
Without a light
Upon an arc of white.
If ruff it was of dame
Or shroud of gnome,
Himself, himself inform.
Of immortality
His strategy
Was physiognomy.

## XII

THE wind tapped like a tired man,
And like a host, "Come in,"
I boldly answered; entered then
My residence within

A rapid, footless guest,
To offer whom a chair
Were as impossible as hand
A sofa to the air.

No bone had he to bind him,
His speech was like the push
Of numerous humming-birds at once
From a superior bush.

His countenance a billow,
His fingers, if he pass,
Let go a music, as of tunes
Blown tremulous in glass.

He visited, still flitting;
Then, like a timid man,
Again he tapped — 'twas flurriedly —
And I became alone.

## XIII

Nature rarer uses yellow
   Than another hue;
Saves she all of that for sunsets, —
   Prodigal of blue,

Spending scarlet like a woman,
   Yellow she affords
Only scantly and selectly,
   Like a lover's words.

## XIV

How happy is the little stone
That rambles in the road alone,
And doesn't care about careers,
And exigencies never fears;
Whose coat of elemental brown
A passing universe put on;
And independent as the sun,
Associates or glows alone,
Fulfilling absolute decree
In casual simplicity.

## XV

THE wind began to rock the grass
With threatening tunes and low, —
He flung a menace at the earth,
A menace at the sky.

The leaves unhooked themselves from trees
And started all abroad;
The dust did scoop itself like hands
And throw away the road.

The wagons quickened on the streets,
The thunder hurried slow;
The lightning showed a yellow beak,
And then a livid claw.

The birds put up the bars to nests,
The cattle fled to barns;
There came one drop of giant rain,
And then, as if the hands

That held the dams had parted hold,
The waters wrecked the sky,
But overlooked my father's house,
Just quartering a tree.

## XVI

SHE sweeps with many-colored brooms,
And leaves the shreds behind;
Oh, housewife in the evening west,
Come back, and dust the pond!

You dropped a purple ravelling in,
You dropped an amber thread;
And now you've littered all the East
With duds of emerald!

And still she plies her spotted brooms,
And still the aprons fly,
Till brooms fade softly into stars —
And then I come away.

## XVII

WHERE ships of purple gently toss
On seas of daffodil,
Fantastic sailors mingle,
And then — the wharf is still.

## XVIII

*A*s imperceptibly as grief
The summer lapsed away, —
Too imperceptible, at last,
To seem like perfidy.

A quietness distilled,
As twilight long begun,
Or Nature, spending with herself
Sequestered afternoon.

The dusk drew earlier in,
The morning foreign shone, —
A courteous, yet harrowing grace,
As guest who would be gone.

And thus, without a wing,
Or service of a keel,
Our summer made her light escape
Into the beautiful.

## XIX

$G$OD made a little gentian;
It tried to be a rose
And failed, and all the summer laughed.
But just before the snows
There came a purple creature
That ravished all the hill;
And summer hid her forehead,
And mockery was still.
The frosts were her condition;
The Tyrian would not come
Until the North evoked it.
"Creator! shall I bloom?"

## XX

$I$T sifts from leaden sieves,
It powders all the wood,
It fills with alabaster wool
The wrinkles of the road.

It makes an even face
Of mountain and of plain, —
Unbroken forehead from the east
Unto the east again.

It reaches to the fence,
It wraps it, rail by rail,
Till it is lost in fleeces;
It flings a crystal veil

On stump and stack and stem, —
The summer's empty room,
Acres of seams where harvests were,
Recordless, but for them.

It ruffles wrists of posts,
As ankles of a queen, —
Then stills its artisans like ghosts,
Denying they have been.

## XXI

THE pedigree of honey
Does not concern the bee;
A clover, any time, to him
Is aristocracy.

## XXII

SOME keep the Sabbath going to church;
I keep it staying at home,
With a bobolink for a chorister,
And an orchard for a dome.

Some keep the Sabbath in surplice;
I just wear my wings,
And instead of tolling the bell for church,
Our little sexton sings.

God preaches, — a noted clergyman, —
And the sermon is never long;
So instead of getting to heaven at last,
I'm going all along!

## XXIII

$\mathcal{A}$ LITTLE road not made of man,
Enabled of the eye,
Accessible to thill of bee,
Or cart of butterfly.

If town it have, beyond itself,
'Tis that I cannot say;
I only sigh, — no vehicle
Bears me along that way.

## XXIV

$\mathcal{A}$ DROP fell on the apple tree,
Another on the roof;
A half a dozen kissed the eaves,
And made the gables laugh.

A few went out to help the brook,
That went to help the sea.
Myself conjectured, Were they pearls,
What necklaces could be!

The dust replaced in hoisted roads,
The birds jocoser sung;
The sunshine threw his hat away,
The orchards spangles hung.

The breezes brought dejected lutes,
And bathed them in the glee;
The East put out a single flag,
And signed the fête away.

## XXV

LIKE trains of cars on tracks of plush
I hear the level bee:
A jar across the flowers goes,
Their velvet masonry

Withstands until the sweet assault
Their chivalry consumes,
While he, victorious, tilts away
To vanquish other blooms.

His feet are shod with gauze,
His helmet is of gold;
His breast, a single onyx
With chrysoprase, inlaid.

His labor is a chant,
His idleness a tune;
Oh, for a bee's experience
Of clovers and of noon!

## XXVI

PRESENTIMENT is that long shadow on the lawn
Indicative that suns go down;
The notice to the startled grass
That darkness is about to pass.

## XXVII

So bashful when I spied her,
So pretty, so ashamed!
So hidden in her leaflets,
Lest anybody find;

So breathless till I passed her,
So helpless when I turned
And bore her, struggling, blushing,
Her simple haunts beyond!

For whom I robbed the dingle,
For whom betrayed the dell,
Many will doubtless ask me,
But I shall never tell!

## XXVIII

$\mathcal{I}$'LL tell you how the sun rose, —
A ribbon at a time.
The steeples swam in amethyst,
The news like squirrels ran.

The hills untied their bonnets,
The bobolinks begun.
Then I said softly to myself,
"That must have been the sun!"

But how he set, I know not.
There seemed a purple stile
Which little yellow boys and girls
Were climbing all the while

Till when they reached the other side,
A dominie in gray
Put gently up the evening bars,
And led the flock away.

## XXIX

OF all the sounds despatched abroad,
There's not a charge to me
Like that old measure in the boughs,
That phraseless melody

The wind does, working like a hand
Whose fingers comb the sky,
Then quiver down, with tufts of tune
Permitted gods and me.

When winds go round and round in bands,
And thrum upon the door,
And birds take places overhead,
To bear them orchestra,

I crave him grace, of summer boughs,
If such an outcast be,
He never heard that fleshless chant
Rise solemn in the tree,

As if some caravan of sound
On deserts, in the sky,
Had broken rank,
Then knit, and passed
In seamless company.

### XXX

$\mathcal{A}$PPARENTLY with no surprise
To any happy flower,
The frost beheads it at its play
In accidental power.

The blond assassin passes on,
The sun proceeds unmoved
To measure off another day
For an approving God.

## XXXI

THESE are the days when birds come back,
A very few, a bird or two,
To take a backward look.

These are the days when skies put on
The old, old sophistries of June, —
A blue and gold mistake.

Graduation

Oh, fraud that cannot cheat the bee,
Almost thy plausibility
Induces my belief,

Till ranks of seeds their witness bear,
And softly through the altered air
Hurries a timid leaf!

Oh, sacrament of summer days,
Oh, last communion in the haze,
Permit a child to join,

Thy sacred emblems to partake,
Thy consecrated bread to break,
Taste thine immortal wine!

## XXXII

THE sky is low, the clouds are mean,
A travelling flake of snow
Across a barn or through a rut
Debates if it will go.

A narrow wind complains all day
How some one treated him;
Nature, like us, is sometimes caught
Without her diadem.

## XXXIII

*T*HERE'S a certain slant of light,
On winter afternoons,
That oppresses, like the weight
Of cathedral tunes.

Heavenly hurt it gives us;
We can find no scar,
But internal difference
Where the meanings are.

None may teach it anything,
'Tis the seal, despair, —
An imperial affliction
Sent us of the air.

When it comes, the landscape listens,
Shadows hold their breath;
When it goes, 'tis like the distance
On the look of death.

## XXXIV

*A* LIGHT exists in spring
   Not present on the year
At any other period.
   When March is scarcely here

A color stands abroad
   On solitary hills
That science cannot overtake,
   But human nature feels.

It waits upon the lawn;
   It shows the furthest tree
Upon the furthest slope we know;
   It almost speaks to me.

Then, as horizons step,
   Or noons report away,
Without the formula of sound,
   It passes, and we stay:

A quality of loss
 Affecting our content,
As trade had suddenly encroached
 Upon a sacrament.

## XXXV

*A* LADY red upon the hill
 Her annual secret keeps;
A lady white within the field
 In placid lily sleeps!

The tidy breezes with their brooms
 Sweep vale, and hill, and tree!
Prithee, my pretty housewives!
 Who may expected be?

The neighbors do not yet suspect!
 The woods exchange a smile —
Orchard, and buttercup, and bird —
 In such a little while!

And yet how still the landscape stands,
How nonchalant the wood,
As if the resurrection
Were nothing very odd!

## XXXVI

*D*EAR March, come in!
How glad I am!
I looked for you before.
Put down your hat —
You must have walked —
How out of breath you are!
Dear March, how are you?
And the rest?
Did you leave Nature well?
Oh, March, come right upstairs with me,
I have so much to tell!

I got your letter, and the bird's;
The maples never knew
That you were coming, — I declare,
How red their faces grew!
But, March, forgive me —
And all those hills
You left for me to hue;
There was no purple suitable,
You took it all with you.

Who knocks?  That April!
Lock the door!
I will not be pursued!
He stayed away a year, to call
When I am occupied.
But trifles look so trivial
As soon as you have come,
That blame is just as dear as praise
And praise as mere as blame.

## XXXVII

*W*E like March, his shoes are purple,
　　He is new and high;
Makes he mud for dog and peddler,
　　Makes he forest dry;
Knows the adder's tongue his coming,
　　And begets her spot.
Stands the sun so close and mighty
　　That our minds are hot.
News is he of all the others;
　　Bold it were to die
With the blue-birds buccaneering
　　On his British sky.

## XXXVIII

*N*OT knowing when the dawn will come
　　I open every door;
Or has it feathers like a bird,
　　Or billows like a shore?

XXXIX

*A* MURMUR in the trees to note,
  Not loud enough for wind;
A star not far enough to seek,
  Nor near enough to find;

A long, long yellow on the lawn,
  A hubbub as of feet;
Not audible, as ours to us,
  But dapperer, more sweet;

A hurrying home of little men
  To houses unperceived, —
All this, and more, if I should tell,
  Would never be believed.

Of robins in the trundle bed
  How many I espy
Whose nightgowns could not hide the wings,
  Although I heard them try!

But then I promised ne'er to tell;
How could I break my word?
So go your way and I'll go mine, —
No fear you'll miss the road.

## XL

To my quick ear the leaves conferred;
The bushes they were bells;
I could not find a privacy
From Nature's sentinels.

In cave if I presumed to hide,
The walls began to tell;
Creation seemed a mighty crack
To make me visible.

## XLI

A SEPAL, petal, and a thorn
Upon a common summer's morn,
A flash of dew, a bee or two,

A breeze
A caper in the trees, —
  And I'm a rose!


## XLII

*W*HAT mystery pervades a well!
  The water lives so far,
Like neighbor from another world
  Residing in a jar.

The grass does not appear afraid;
  I often wonder he
Can stand so close and look so bold
  At what is dread to me.

Related somehow they may be, —
  The sedge stands next the sea,
Where he is floorless, yet of fear
  No evidence gives he.

But nature is a stranger yet;
The ones that cite her most
Have never passed her haunted house,
Nor simplified her ghost.

To pity those that know her not
Is helped by the regret
That those who know her, know her less
The nearer her they get.

## XLIII

To make a prairie it takes a clover
and one bee, —
One clover, and a bee,
And revery.
The revery alone will do
If bees are few.

## XLIV

IT'S like the light, —
  A fashionless delight,
It's like the bee, —
  A dateless melody.

It's like the woods,
  Private like breeze,
Phraseless, yet it stirs
  The proudest trees.

It's like the morning, —
  Best when it's done, —
The everlasting clocks
  Chime noon.

## XLV

COULD I but ride indefinite,
　　As doth the meadow-bee,
And visit only where I liked,
　　And no man visit me,

And flirt all day with buttercups,
　　And marry whom I may,
And dwell a little everywhere,
　　Or better, run away

With no police to follow,
　　Or chase me if I do,
Till I should jump peninsulas
　　To get away from you, —

I said, but just to be a bee
　　Upon a raft of air,
And row in nowhere all day long,
　　And anchor off the bar, —
What liberty!  So captives deem
　　Who tight in dungeons are.

## XLVI

THE moon was but a chin of gold
  A night or two ago,
And now she turns her perfect face
  Upon the world below.

Her forehead is of amplest blond;
  Her cheek like beryl stone;
Her eye unto the summer dew
  The likest I have known.

Her lips of amber never part;
  But what must be the smile
Upon her friend she could bestow
  Were such her silver will!

And what a privilege to be
  But the remotest star!
For certainly her way might pass
  Beside your twinkling door.

Her bonnet is the firmament,
    The universe her shoe,
The stars the trinkets at her belt,
    Her dimities of blue.

## XLVII

THE bat is dun with wrinkled wings
    Like fallow article,
And not a song pervades his lips,
    Or none perceptible.

His small umbrella, quaintly halved,
    Describing in the air
An arc alike inscrutable, —
    Elate philosopher!

Deputed from what firmament
    Of what astute abode,
Empowered with what malevolence
    Auspiciously withheld.

To his adroit Creator
  Ascribe no less the praise;
Beneficent, believe me,
  His eccentricities.


## XLVIII

*Y*OU'VE seen balloons set, haven't you?
  So stately they ascend
It is as swans discarded you
  For duties diamond.

Their liquid feet go softly out
  Upon a sea of blond;
They spurn the air as 'twere to mean
  For creatures so renowned.

Their ribbons just beyond the eye,
  They struggle some for breath,
And yet the crowd applauds below;
  They would not encore death.

The gilded creature strains and spins,
    Trips frantic in a tree,
Tears open her imperial veins
    And tumbles in the sea.

The crowd retire with an oath
    The dust in streets goes down,
And clerks in counting-rooms observe,
    "'Twas only a balloon."

### XLIX

THE cricket sang,
And set the sun,
And workmen finished, one by one,
    Their seam the day upon.

The low grass loaded with the dew,
The twilight stood as strangers do
With hat in hand, polite and new,
    To stay as if, or go.

A vastness, as a neighbor, came, —
A wisdom without face or name,
A peace, as hemispheres at home, —
  And so the night became.


## L

*D*RAB habitation of whom?
  Tabernacle or tomb,
Or dome of worm,
Or porch of gnome,
Or some elf's catacomb?

(Sent with a cocoon to her little nephew.)


## LI

*O*F bronze and blaze
The north, to-night!
  So adequate its forms,
So preconcerted with itself,
  So distant to alarms, —

101

An unconcern so sovereign
　　To universe, or me,
It paints my simple spirit
　　With tints of majesty,
Till I take vaster attitudes,
　　And strut upon my stem,
Disdaining men and oxygen,
　　For arrogance of them.

My splendors are menagerie;
　　But their completeless show
Will entertain the centuries
　　When I am, long ago,
An island in dishonored grass,
　　Whom none but daisies know.

## LII

How the old mountains drip with sunset,
　　And the brake of dun!
How the hemlocks are tipped in tinsel
　　By the wizard sun!

How the old steeples hand the scarlet,
   Till the ball is full, —
Have I the lip of the flamingo
   That I dare to tell?

Then, how the fire ebbs like billows,
   Touching all the grass
With a departing, sapphire feature,
   As if a duchess pass!

How a small dusk crawls on the village
   Till the houses blot;
And the odd flambeaux no men carry
   Glimmer on the spot!

Now it is night in nest and kennel,
   And where was the wood,
Just a dome of abyss is nodding
   Into solitude! —

These are the visions baffled Guido;
   Titian never told;
Domenichino dropped the pencil,
   Powerless to unfold.

# PART THREE

*Love*

*It's all I have to bring to-day,*

*This, and my heart beside,*

*This, and my heart, and all the fields,*

*And all the meadows wide.*

*Be sure you count, should I forget, —*

*Some one the sun could tell, —*

*This, and my heart, and all the bees*

*Which in the clover dwell.*

## I

*Y*OU left me, sweet, two legacies, —
A legacy of love
A Heavenly Father would content,
Had He the offer of;

You left me boundaries of pain
Capacious as the sea,
Between eternity and time,
Your consciousness and me.

## II

*A*LTER? When the hills do.
Falter? When the sun
Question if his glory
Be the perfect one.

Surfeit? When the daffodil
Doth of the dew:
Even as herself, O friend!
I will of you!

## III

ELYSIUM is as far as to
The very nearest room,
If in that room a friend await
Felicity or doom.

What fortitude the soul contains,
That it can so endure
The accent of a coming foot,
The opening of a door!

## IV

IF you were coming in the fall,
I'd brush the summer by
With half a smile and half a spurn,
As housewives do a fly.

If I could see you in a year,
I'd wind the months in balls,
And put them each in separate drawers,
Until their time befalls.

If only centuries delayed,
I'd count them on my hand,
Subtracting till my fingers dropped
Into Van Diemen's land.

If certain, when this life was out,
That yours and mine should be,
I'd toss it yonder like a rind,
And taste eternity.

But now, all ignorant of the length
Of time's uncertain wing,
It goads me, like the goblin bee,
That will not state its sting.

## V

*I* HIDE myself within my flower,
That wearing on your breast,
You, unsuspecting, wear me too —
And angels know the rest.

I hide myself within my flower,
That, fading from your vase,
You, unsuspecting, feel for me
Almost a loneliness.

## VI

*I* CANNOT live with you,
It would be life,
And life is over there
Behind the shelf

The sexton keeps the key to,
Putting up
Our life, his porcelain,
Like a cup

Discarded of the housewife,
Quaint or broken;
A newer Sèvres pleases,
Old ones crack.

I could not die with you,
For one must wait
To shut the other's gaze down, —
You could not.

And I, could I stand by
And see you freeze,
Without my right of frost,
Death's privilege?

Nor could I rise with you,
Because your face
Would put out Jesus',
That new grace

Glow plain and foreign
On my homesick eye,
Except that you, than he
Shone closer by.

They'd judge us — how?
For you served Heaven, you know,
Or sought to;
I could not,

Because you saturated sight,
And I had no more eyes
For sordid excellence
As Paradise.

And were you lost, I would be,
Though my name
Rang loudest
On the heavenly fame.

And were you saved,
And I condemned to be

Where you were not,
That self were hell to me.

So we must keep apart,
You there, I here,
With just the door ajar
That oceans are,
And prayer,
And that pale sustenance,
Despair!

## VII

THERE came a day at summer's full
Entirely for me;
I thought that such were for the saints,
Where revelations be.

The sun, as common, went abroad,
The flowers, accustomed, blew,
As if no sail the solstice passed
That maketh all things new.

The time was scarce profaned by speech;
The symbol of a word
Was needless, as at sacrament
The wardrobe of our Lord.

Each was to each the sealed church,
Permitted to commune this time,
Lest we too awkward show
At supper of the Lamb.

The hours slid fast, as hours will,
Clutched tight by greedy hands;
So faces on two decks look back,
Bound to opposing lands.

And so, when all the time had failed,
Without external sound,
Each bound the other's crucifix,
We gave no other bond.

Sufficient troth that we shall rise —
Deposed, at length, the grave —
To that new marriage, justified
Through Calvaries of Love!

## VIII

I'M ceded, I've stopped being theirs;
The name they dropped upon my face
With water, in the country church,
Is finished using now,

And they can put it with my dolls,
My childhood, and the string of spools
I've finished threading too.

Baptized before without the choice,
But this time consciously, of grace
Unto supremest name,
Called to my full, the crescent dropped,
Existence's whole arc filled up
With one small diadem.

My second rank, too small the first,
Crowned, crowing on my father's breast,
A half unconscious queen;
But this time, adequate, erect,
With will to choose or to reject,
And I choose — just a throne.

## IX

$\mathcal{I}$'M wife; I've finished that,
That other state;
I'm Czar, I'm woman now:
It's safer so.

How odd the girl's life looks
Behind this soft eclipse!
I think that earth seems so
To those in heaven now.

This being comfort, then
That other kind was pain;
But why compare?
I'm wife! stop there!

## X

SHE rose to his requirement, dropped
The playthings of her life
To take the honorable work
Of woman and of wife.

If aught she missed in her new day
Of amplitude, or awe,
Or first prospective, or the gold
In using wore away,

It lay unmentioned, as the sea
Develops pearl and weed,
But only to himself is known
The fathoms they abide.

## XI

COME slowly, Eden!
Lips unused to thee,
Bashful, sip thy jasmines,
As the fainting bee,

Reaching late his flower,
Round her chamber hums,
Counts his nectars — enters
And is lost in balms!

## XII

OF all the souls that stand create
I have elected one.
When sense from spirit files away,
And subterfuge is done;

When that which is and that which was
Apart, intrinsic, stand,
And this brief tragedy of flesh
Is shifted like a sand;

When figures show their royal front
And mists are carved away, —
Behold the atom I preferred
To all the lists of clay!

## XIII

*Y*OUR riches taught me poverty.
Myself a millionnaire
In little wealths, — as girls could boast, —
Till broad as Buenos Ayre,

You drifted your dominions
A different Peru;
And I esteemed all poverty,
For life's estate with you.

Of mines I little know, myself,
But just the names of gems, —
The colors of the commonest;
And scarce of diadems

So much that, did I meet the queen,
Her glory I should know:
But this must be a different wealth,
To miss it beggars so.

I'm sure 'tis India all day
To those who look on you
Without a stint, without a blame, —
Might I but be the Jew!

I'm sure it is Golconda,
Beyond my power to deem, —
To have a smile for mine each day,
How better than a gem!

At least, it solaces to know
That there exists a gold,
Although I prove it just in time
Its distance to behold!

It's far, far treasure to surmise,
And estimate the pearl
That slipped my simple fingers through
While just a girl at school!

## XIV

$\mathcal{I}$ GAVE myself to him,
And took himself for pay.
The solemn contract of a life
Was ratified this way.

The wealth might disappoint,
Myself a poorer prove
Than this great purchaser suspect,
The daily own of Love

Depreciate the vision;
But, till the merchant buy,
Still fable, in the isles of spice,
The subtle cargoes lie.

At least, 'tis mutual risk, —
Some found it mutual gain;
Sweet debt of Life, — each night to owe,
Insolvent, every noon.

## XV

$G$OING to him!  Happy letter!  Tell him —
Tell him the page I didn't write;
Tell him I only said the syntax,
And left the verb and the pronoun out.
Tell him just how the fingers hurried,
Then how they waded, slow, slow, slow;
And then you wished you had eyes in your pages,
So you could see what moved them so.

"Tell him it wasn't a practised writer,
You guessed, from the way the sentence toiled;
You could hear the bodice tug, behind you,
As if it held but the might of a child;
You almost pitied it, you, it worked so.
Tell him — No, you may quibble there,
For it would split his heart to know it,
And then you and I were silenter.

"Tell him night finished before we finished,
And the old clock kept neighing 'day!'
And you got sleepy and begged to be ended —
What could it hinder so, to say?
Tell him just how she sealed you, cautious,
But if he ask where you are hid
Until to-morrow, — happy letter!
Gesture, coquette, and shake your head!"


## XVI

WILD nights! Wild nights!
Were I with thee,
Wild nights should be
Our luxury!

Futile the winds
To a heart in port, —
Done with the compass,
Done with the chart.

Rowing in Eden!
Ah! the sea!
Might I but moor
To-night in thee!

## XVII

*D*ID the harebell loose her girdle
To the lover bee,
Would the bee the harebell hallow
Much as formerly?

Did the paradise, persuaded,
Yield her moat of pearl,
Would the Eden be an Eden,
Or the earl an earl?

## XVIII

*A* CHARM invests a face
Imperfectly beheld, —
The lady dare not lift her veil
For fear it be dispelled.

But peers beyond her mesh,
And wishes, and denies, —
Lest interview annul a want
That image satisfies.

## XIX

*I* HELD a jewel in my fingers
And went to sleep.
The day was warm, and winds were prosy;
I said: " 'Twill keep."

I woke and chid my honest fingers, —
The gem was gone;
And now an amethyst remembrance
Is all I own.

## XX

$\mathcal{P}$ROUD of my broken heart since thou didst
   break it,
     Proud of the pain I did not feel till thee,
Proud of my night since thou with moons dost
   slake it,
     Not to partake thy passion, my humility.

## XXI

$\mathcal{M}$Y worthiness is all my doubt,
    His merit all my fear,
Contrasting which, my qualities
    Do lowlier appear;

Lest I should insufficient prove
    For his beloved need,
The chiefest apprehension
    Within my loving creed.

So I, the undivine abode
    Of his elect content,

Conform my soul as 'twere a church
Unto her sacrament.

## XXII

$\mathcal{L}$OVE is anterior to life,
Posterior to death,
Initial of creation, and
The exponent of breath.

## XXIII

$\mathcal{W}$HEN roses cease to bloom, dear,
And violets are done,
When bumble-bees in solemn flight
Have passed beyond the sun,

The hand that paused to gather
Upon this summer's day
Will idle lie, in Auburn, —
Then take my flower, pray!

## XXIV

SUMMER for thee grant I may be
When summer days are flown!
Thy music still when whippoorwill
And oriole are done!

For thee to bloom, I'll skip the tomb
And sow my blossoms o'er!
Pray gather me, Anemone,
Thy flower forevermore!

## XXV

SPLIT the lark and you'll find the music,
Bulb after bulb, in silver rolled,
Scantily dealt to the summer morning,
Saved for your ear when lutes be old.

Loose the flood, you shall find it patent,
Gush after gush, reserved for you;
Scarlet experiment! sceptic Thomas,
Now, do you doubt that your bird was true?

## XXVI

To lose thee, sweeter than to gain
    All other hearts I knew.
'Tis true the drought is destitute,
    But then I had the dew!

The Caspian has its realms of sand,
    Its other realm of sea;
Without the sterile perquisite
    No Caspian could be.

## XXVII

POOR little heart!
    Did they forget thee?
Then dinna care! Then dinna care!

    Proud little heart!
        Did they forsake thee?
Be debonair! Be debonair!

Frail little heart!
I would not break thee:
Could'st credit me? Could'st credit me?

Gay little heart!
Like morning glory
Thou'll wilted be; thou'll wilted be!

## XXVIII

THERE is a word
   Which bears a sword
   Can pierce an armed man.
It hurls its barbed syllables, —
   At once is mute again.
But where it fell
The saved will tell
   On patriotic day,
Some epauletted brother
   Gave his breath away.

Wherever runs the breathless sun,
　　Wherever roams the day,
There is its noiseless onset,
　　There is its victory!
Behold the keenest marksman!
　　The most accomplished shot!
Time's sublimest target
　　Is a soul "forgot"!

## XXIX

*I*'VE got an arrow here;
　　Loving the hand that sent it,
I the dart revere.

Fell, they will say, in "skirmish"!
　　Vanquished, my soul will know,
By but a simple arrow
　　Sped by an archer's bow.

## XXX

HE fumbles at your spirit
   As players at the keys
Before they drop full music on;
   He stuns you by degrees,

Prepares your brittle substance
   For the ethereal blow,
By fainter hammers, further heard,
   Then nearer, then so slow

Your breath has time to straighten,
   Your brain to bubble cool, —
Deals one imperial thunderbolt
   That scalps your naked soul.

## XXXI

HEART, we will forget him!
    You and I, to-night!
You may forget the warmth he gave,
    I will forget the light.

When you have done, pray tell me,
    That I my thoughts may dim;
Haste! lest while you're lagging,
    I may remember him!

## XXXII

FATHER, I bring thee not myself, —
    That were the little load;
I bring thee the imperial heart
    I had not strength to hold.

The heart I cherished in my own
    Till mine too heavy grew,
Yet strangest, heavier since it went,
    Is it too large for you?

## XXXIII

*W*E outgrow love like other things
And put it in the drawer,
Till it an antique fashion shows
Like costumes grandsires wore.

## XXXIV

*N*OT with a club the heart is broken,
Nor with a stone;
A whip, so small you could not see it,
I've known

To lash the magic creature
Till it fell,
Yet that whip's name too noble
Then to tell.

Magnanimous of bird
By boy descried,
To sing unto the stone
Of which it died.

## XXXV

HE touched me, so I live to know
That such a day, permitted so,
  I groped upon his breast.
It was a boundless place to me,
And silenced, as the awful sea
  Puts minor streams to rest.

And now, I'm different from before,
As if I breathed superior air,
  Or brushed a royal gown;
My feet, too, that had wandered so,
My gypsy face transfigured now
  To tenderer renown.

## XXXVI

LET me not mar that perfect dream
  By an auroral stain,
But so adjust my daily night
  That it will come again.

## XXXVII

$\mathcal{I}$ LIVE with him, I see his face;
   I go no more away
For visitor, or sundown;
   Death's single privacy,

The only one forestalling mine,
   And that by right that he
Presents a claim invisible,
   No wedlock granted me.

I live with him, I hear his voice,
   I stand alive to-day
To witness to the certainty
   Of immortality

Taught me by Time, — the lower way,
   Conviction every day, —
That life like this is endless,
   Be judgment what it may.

## XXXVIII

*I* ENVY seas whereon he rides,
    I envy spokes of wheels
Of chariots that him convey,
    I envy speechless hills

That gaze upon his journey;
    How easy all can see
What is forbidden utterly
    As heaven, unto me!

I envy nests of sparrows
    That dot his distant eaves,
The wealthy fly upon his pane,
    The happy, happy leaves

That just abroad his window
    Have summer's leave to be,
The earrings of Pizarro
    Could not obtain for me.

I envy light that wakes him,
  And bells that boldly ring
To tell him it is noon abroad, —
  Myself his noon could bring,

Yet interdict my blossom
  And abrogate my bee,
Lest noon in everlasting night
  Drop Gabriel and me.

## XXXIX

*A* SOLEMN thing it was, I said,
  A woman white to be,
And wear, if God should count me fit,
  Her hallowed mystery.

A timid thing to drop a life
  Into the purple well,
Too plummetless that it come back
  Eternity until.

# PART FOUR

# Time and Eternity

The daisy follows soft the sun,
And when his golden walk is done,
    Sits shyly at his feet.
He, waking, finds the flower near.
"Wherefore, marauder, art thou here?"
    "Because, sir, love is sweet!"

We are the flower, Thou the sun!
Forgive us, if as days decline,
    We nearer steal to Thee, —
Enamoured of the parting west,
The peace, the flight, the amethyst,
    Night's possibility!

## I

SAFE in their alabaster chambers,
Untouched by morning and untouched by noon,
Sleep the meek members of the resurrection,
Rafter of satin, and roof of stone.

Light laughs the breeze in her castle of sunshine;
Babbles the bee in a stolid ear;
Pipe the sweet birds in ignorant cadence, —
Ah, what sagacity perished here!

Grand go the years in the crescent above them;
Worlds scoop their arcs, and firmaments row,
Diadems drop and Doges surrender,
Soundless as dots on a disk of snow.

## II

EXULTATION is the going
Of an inland soul to sea, —
Past the houses, past the headlands,
Into deep eternity!

Bred as we, among the mountains,
Can the sailor understand
The divine intoxication
Of the first league out from land?

## III

LOOK back on time with kindly eyes,
He doubtless did his best;
How softly sinks his trembling sun
In human nature's west!

## IV

I DIED for beauty, but was scarce
Adjusted in the tomb,
When one who died for truth was lain
In an adjoining room.

He questioned softly why I failed?
"For beauty," I replied.
"And I for truth, — the two are one;
We brethren are," he said.

And so, as kinsmen met a night,
We talked between the rooms,
Until the moss had reached our lips,
And covered up our names.

### V

*I* LIKE a look of agony,
Because I know it's true;
Men do not sham convulsion,
Nor simulate a throe.

The eyes glaze once, and that is death.
Impossible to feign
The beads upon the forehead
By homely anguish strung.

## VI

*I*'VE seen a dying eye
Run round and round a room
In search of something, as it seemed,
Then cloudier become;
And then, obscure with fog,
And then be soldered down,
Without disclosing what it be,
'Twere blessed to have seen.

## VII

*I* NEVER saw a moor,
I never saw the sea;
Yet know I how the heather looks,
And what a wave must be.

I never spoke with God,
Nor visited in heaven;
Yet certain am I of the spot
As if the chart were given.

## VIII

$\mathcal{G}$OD permits industrious angels
Afternoons to play.
I met one, — forgot my school-mates,
All, for him, straightway.

God calls home the angels promptly
At the setting sun;
I missed mine. How dreary marbles,
After playing Crown!

## IX

$\mathcal{T}$HE last night that she lived,
It was a common night,
Except the dying; this to us
Made nature different.

We noticed smallest things, —
Things overlooked before,
By this great light upon our minds
Italicized, as 'twere.

That others could exist
While she must finish quite,
A jealousy for her arose
So nearly infinite.

We waited while she passed;
It was a narrow time,
Too jostled were our souls to speak,
At length the notice came.

She mentioned, and forgot;
Then lightly as a reed
Bent to the water, shivered scarce,
Consented, and was dead.

And we, we placed the hair,
And drew the head erect;
And then an awful leisure was,
Our faith to regulate.

## X

NOT in this world to see his face
Sounds long, until I read the place
Where this is said to be
But just the primer to a life
Unopened, rare, upon the shelf,
Clasped yet to him and me.

And yet, my primer suits me so
I would not choose a book to know
Than that, be sweeter wise;
Might some one else so learned be,
And leave me just my A B C,
Himself could have the skies.

## XI

THE bustle in a house
The morning after death
Is solemnest of industries
Enacted upon earth, —

The sweeping up the heart,
And putting love away
We shall not want to use again
Until eternity.

## XII

BECAUSE I could not stop for Death,
He kindly stopped for me;
The carriage held but just ourselves
And Immortality.

We slowly drove, he knew no haste,
And I had put away
My labor, and my leisure too,
For his civility.

We passed the school where children played
At wrestling in a ring;
We passed the fields of gazing grain,
We passed the setting sun.

We paused before a house that seemed
A swelling of the ground;
The roof was scarcely visible,
The cornice but a mound.

Since then 'tis centuries; but each
Feels shorter than the day
I first surmised the horses' heads
Were toward eternity.

### XIII

DEATH is a dialogue between
The spirit and the dust.
"Dissolve," says Death. The Spirit, "Sir,
I have another trust."

Death doubts it, argues from the ground.
The Spirit turns away,
Just laying off, for evidence,
An overcoat of clay.

## XIV

*I* NEVER lost as much but twice,
And that was in the sod;
Twice have I stood a beggar
Before the door of God!

Angels, twice descending,
Reimbursed my store.
Burglar, banker, father,
I am poor once more!

## XV

*I* HAVE not told my garden yet,
Lest that should conquer me;
I have not quite the strength now
To break it to the bee.

I will not name it in the street,
For shops would stare, that I,
So shy, so very ignorant,
Should have the face to die.

The hillsides must not know it,
Where I have rambled so,
Nor tell the loving forests
The day that I shall go,

Nor lisp it at the table,
Nor heedless by the way
Hint that within the riddle
One will walk to-day!

## XVI

DEATH sets a thing significant
The eye had hurried by,
Except a perished creature
Entreat us tenderly

To ponder little workmanships
In crayon or in wool,
With "This was last her fingers did,"
Industrious until

The thimble weighed too heavy,
The stitches stopped themselves,
And then 'twas put among the dust
Upon the closet shelves.

A book I have, a friend gave,
Whose pencil, here and there,
Had notched the place that pleased him, —
At rest his fingers are.

Now, when I read, I read not,
For interrupting tears
Obliterate the etchings
Too costly for repairs.

## XVII

*I* WENT to heaven, —
'Twas a small town,
Lit with a ruby,
Lathed with down.
Stiller than the fields
At the full dew,

Beautiful as pictures
No man drew.
People like the moth,
Of mechlin, frames,
Duties of gossamer,
And eider names.
Almost contented
I could be
'Mong such unique
Society.

## XVIII

OUR journey had advanced;
Our feet were almost come
To that odd fork in Being's road,
Eternity by term.

Our pace took sudden awe,
Our feet reluctant led.
Before were cities, but between,
The forest of the dead.

Retreat was out of hope, —
Behind, a sealed route,
Eternity's white flag before,
And God at every gate.

### XIX

$\mathcal{I}$ LIVED on dread; to those who know
The stimulus there is
In danger, other impetus
Is numb and vital-less.

As 'twere a spur upon the soul,
A fear will urge it where
To go without the spectre's aid
Were challenging despair.

## XX

*H*ER final summer was it,
And yet we guessed it not;
If tenderer industriousness
Pervaded her, we thought

A further force of life
Developed from within, —
When Death lit all the shortness up,
And made the hurry plain.

We wondered at our blindness, —
When nothing was to see
But her Carrara guide-post, —
At our stupidity,

When, duller than our dulness,
The busy darling lay,
So busy was she, finishing,
So leisurely were we!

## XXI

ONE need not be a chamber to be haunted,
One need not be a house;
The brain has corridors surpassing
Material place.

Far safer, of a midnight meeting
External ghost,
Than an interior confronting
That whiter host.

Far safer through an Abbey gallop,
The stones achase,
Than, moonless, one's own self encounter
In lonesome place.

Ourself, behind ourself concealed,
Should startle most;
Assassin, hid in our apartment,
Be horror's least.

The prudent carries a revolver,
He bolts the door,
O'erlooking a superior spectre
More near.

## XXII

IT was not death, for I stood up,
And all the dead lie down;
It was not night, for all the bells
Put out their tongues, for noon.

It was not frost, for on my flesh
I felt siroccos crawl, —
Nor fire, for just my marble feet
Could keep a chancel cool.

And yet it tasted like them all;
The figures I have seen
Set orderly, for burial,
Reminded me of mine,

As if my life were shaven
And fitted to a frame,
And could not breathe without a key;
And 'twas like midnight, some,

When everything that ticked has stopped,
And space stares, all around,
Or grisly frosts, first autumn morns,
Repeal the beating ground.

But most like chaos, — stopless, cool, —
Without a chance or spar,
Or even a report of land
To justify despair.

## XXIII

*G*REAT streets of silence led away
To neighborhoods of pause;
Here was no notice, no dissent,
No universe, no laws.

By clocks 'twas morning, and for night
The bells at distance called;
But epoch had no basis here,
For period exhaled.

## XXIV

*A*FTER a hundred years
Nobody knows the place, —
Agony, that enacted there,
Motionless as peace.

Weeds triumphant ranged,
Strangers strolled and spelled
At the lone orthography
Of the elder dead.

Winds of summer fields
Recollect the way, —
Instinct picking up the key
Dropped by memory.

## XXV

THIS world is not conclusion;
    A sequel stands beyond,
Invisible, as music,
    But positive, as sound.
It beckons and it baffles;
    Philosophies don't know,
And through a riddle, at the last,
    Sagacity must go.
To guess it puzzles scholars;
    To gain it, men have shown
Contempt of generations,
    And crucifixion known.

## XXVI

THEY say that "time assuages", —
    Time never did assuage;
An actual suffering strengthens,
    As sinews do, with age.

Time is a test of trouble,
But not a remedy.
If such it prove, it prove too
There was no malady.

## XXVII

THE distance that the dead have gone
Does not at first appear;
Their coming back seems possible
For many an ardent year.

And then, that we have followed them
We more than half suspect,
So intimate have we become
With their dear retrospect.

## XXVIII

How dare the robins sing,
  When men and women hear
Who since they went to their account
  Have settled with the year! —
Paid all that life had earned
  In one consummate bill,
And now, what life or death can do
  Is immaterial.
Insulting is the sun
  To him whose mortal light,
Beguiled of immortality,
  Bequeaths him to the night.
In deference to him
  Extinct be every hum,
Whose garden wrestles with the dew,
  At daybreak overcome!

## XXIX

DEATH is like the insect
　　Menacing the tree,
Competent to kill it,
　　But decoyed may be.

Bait it with the balsam,
　　Seek it with the knife,
Baffle, if it cost you
　　Everything in life.

Then, if it have burrowed
　　Out of reach of skill,
Ring the tree and leave it, —
　　'Tis the vermin's will.

## XXX

'TIS sunrise, little maid, hast thou
 No station in the day?
'Twas not thy wont to hinder so, —
 Retrieve thine industry.

'Tis noon, my little maid, alas!
 And art thou sleeping yet?
The lily waiting to be wed,
 The bee, dost thou forget?

My little maid, 'tis night; alas,
 That night should be to thee
Instead of morning!  Hadst thou broached
 Thy little plan to me,
Dissuade thee if I could not, sweet,
 I might have aided thee.

## XXXI

*A*s far from pity as complaint,
  As cool to speech as stone,
As numb to revelation
  As if my trade were bone.

As far from time as history,
  As near yourself to-day
As children to the rainbow's scarf,
  Or sunset's yellow play

To eyelids in the sepulchre.
  How still the dancer lies,
While color's revelations break,
  And blaze the butterflies!

## XXXII

SHE laid her docile crescent down,
　　And this mechanic stone
Still states, to dates that have forgot,
　　The news that she is gone.

So constant to its stolid trust,
　　The shaft that never knew,
It shames the constancy that fled
　　Before its emblem flew.

## XXXIII

IMMORTAL is an ample word
　　When what we need is by,
But when it leaves us for a time,
　　'Tis a necessity.

Of heaven above the firmest proof
　　We fundamental know,
Except for its marauding hand,
　　It had been heaven below.

## XXXIV

THIS was in the white of the year,
　That was in the green,
Drifts were as difficult then to think
　As daisies now to be seen.

Looking back is best that is left,
　Or if it be before,
Retrospection is prospect's half,
　Sometimes almost more.

## XXXV

ME! Come! My dazzled face
In such a shining place!

Me! Hear! My foreign ear
The sounds of welcome near!

The saints shall meet
Our bashful feet.

My holiday shall be
That they remember me;

My paradise, the fame
That they pronounce my name.

### XXXVI

From us she wandered now a year,
  Her tarrying unknown;
If wilderness prevent her feet,
  Or that ethereal zone

No eye hath seen and lived,
  We ignorant must be.
We only know what time of year
  We took the mystery.

## XXXVII

BEREAVED of all, I went abroad,
  No less bereaved to be
Upon a new peninsula, —
  The grave preceded me,

Obtained my lodgings ere myself,
  And when I sought my bed,
The grave it was, reposed upon
  The pillow for my head.

I waked, to find it first awake,
  I rose, — it followed me;
I tried to drop it in the crowd,
  To lose it in the sea,

In cups of artificial drowse
  To sleep its shape away, —
The grave was finished, but the spade
  Remained in memory.

## XXXVIII

*I* FELT a funeral in my brain,
 And mourners, to and fro,
Kept treading, treading, till it seemed
 That sense was breaking through.

And when they all were seated,
 A service like a drum
Kept beating, beating, till I thought
 My mind was going numb.

And then I heard them lift a box,
 And creak across my soul
With those same boots of lead, again.
 Then space began to toll

As all the heavens were a bell,
 And Being but an ear,
And I and silence some strange race,
 Wrecked, solitary, here.

## XXXIX

*I* MEANT to find her when I came;
　　Death had the same design;
But the success was his, it seems,
　　And the discomfit mine.

I meant to tell her how I longed
　　For just this single time;
But Death had told her so the first,
　　And she had hearkened him.

To wander now is my abode;
　　To rest, — to rest would be
A privilege of hurricane
　　To memory and me.

## XL

So proud she was to die
　　It made us all ashamed
That what we cherished, so unknown
　　To her desire seemed.

So satisfied to go
　　Where none of us should be,
Immediately, that anguish stooped
　　Almost to jealousy.

## XLI

Tie the strings to my life, my Lord,
　　Then I am ready to go!
Just a look at the horses —
　　Rapid!  That will do!

Put me in on the firmest side,
　　So I shall never fall;
For we must ride to the Judgment,
　　And it's partly down hill.

But never I mind the bridges,
  And never I mind the sea;
Held fast in everlasting race
  By my own choice and thee.

Good-by to the life I used to live,
  And the world I used to know;
And kiss the hills for me, just once;
  Now I am ready to go!


## XLII

THE dying need but little, dear, —
  A glass of water's all,
A flower's unobtrusive face
  To punctuate the wall,

A fan, perhaps, a friend's regret,
  And certainly that one
No color in the rainbow
  Perceives when you are gone.

## XLIII

THE soul should always stand ajar
    That if the heaven inquire,
He will not be obliged to wait,
    Or shy of troubling her.

Depart, before the host has slid
    The bolt upon the door
To seek for the accomplished guest —
    Her visitor no more.

## XLIV

THREE weeks passed since I had seen her, —
    Some disease had vexed;
'Twas with text and village singing
    I beheld her next,

And a company — our pleasure
    To discourse alone;
Gracious now to me as any,
    Gracious unto none.

Borne, without dissent of either,
　To the parish night;
Of the separated people
　Which are out of sight?

## XLV

*I* BREATHED enough to learn the trick,
　And now, removed from air,
I simulate the breath so well,
　That one, to be quite sure

The lungs are stirless, must descend
　Among the cunning cells,
And touch the pantomime himself.
　How cool the bellows feels!

## XLVI

$\mathcal{I}$ HEARD a fly buzz when I died;
  The stillness round my form
Was like the stillness in the air
  Between the heaves of storm.

The eyes beside had wrung them dry,
  And breaths were gathering sure
For that last onset, when the king
  Be witnessed in his power.

I willed my keepsakes, signed away
  What portion of me I
Could make assignable, — and then
  There interposed a fly,

With blue, uncertain, stumbling buzz,
  Between the light and me;
And then the windows failed, and then
  I could not see to see.

## XLVII

ADRIFT! A little boat adrift!
  And night is coming down!
Will no one guide a little boat
  Unto the nearest town?

So sailors say, on yesterday,
  Just as the dusk was brown,
One little boat gave up its strife,
  And gurgled down and down.

But angels say, on yesterday,
  Just as the dawn was red,
One little boat o'erspent with gales
Retrimmed its masts, redecked its sails
  Exultant, onward sped!

## XLVIII

THERE'S been a death in the opposite house
    As lately as to-day.
I know it by the numb look
    Such houses have alway.

The neighbors rustle in and out,
    The doctor drives away.
A window opens like a pod,
    Abrupt, mechanically;

Somebody flings a mattress out, —
    The children hurry by;
They wonder if It died on that, —
    I used to when a boy.

The minister goes stiffly in
    As if the house were his,
And he owned all the mourners now,
    And little boys besides;

And then the milliner, and the man
  Of the appalling trade,
To take the measure of the house.
  There'll be that dark parade

Of tassels and of coaches soon;
  It's easy as a sign, —
The intuition of the news
  In just a country town.


## XLIX

 $\mathcal{I}$T struck me every day
  The lightning was as new
As if the cloud that instant slit
  And let the fire through.

It burned me in the night,
  It blistered in my dream;
It sickened fresh upon my sight
  With every morning's beam.

I thought that storm was brief, —
The maddest, quickest by;
But Nature lost the date of this,
And left it in the sky.


L

*W*ATER is taught by thirst;
Land, by the oceans passed;
Transport, by throe;
Peace, by its battles told;
Love, by memorial mould;
Birds, by the snow.


LI

*A* CLOCK stopped — not the mantel's;
Geneva's farthest skill
Can't put the puppet bowing
That just now dangled still.

An awe came on the trinket!
The figures hunched with pain,

Then quivered out of decimals
    Into degreeless noon.

It will not stir for doctors,
    This pendulum of snow;
The shopman importunes it,
    While cool, concernless No

Nods from the gilded pointers,
    Nods from the seconds slim,
Decades of arrogance between
    The dial life and him.

## LII

ALL overgrown by cunning moss,
    All interspersed with weed,
The little cage of "Currer Bell",
    In quiet Haworth laid.

This bird, observing others,
    When frosts too sharp became,

Retire to other latitudes,
  Quietly did the same.

But differed in returning;
  Since Yorkshire hills are green,
Yet not in all the nests I meet
  Can nightingale be seen.

Gathered from any wanderings,
  Gethsemane can tell
Through what transporting anguish
  She reached the asphodel!

Soft falls the sounds of Eden
  Upon her puzzled ear;
Oh, what an afternoon for heaven,
  When Brontë entered there!

## LIII

*A* TOAD can die of light!
　　Death is the common right
　　Of toads and men, —
Of earl and midge
The privilege.
　　Why swagger then?
The gnat's supremacy
Is large as thine.

## LIV

*A* LONG, long sleep, a famous sleep
　　That makes no show for dawn
By stretch of limb or stir of lid, —
　　An independent one.

Was ever idleness like this?
　　Within a hut of stone
To bask the centuries away
　　Nor once look up for noon?

## LV

'TWAS just this time last year I died.
  I know I heard the corn,
When I was carried by the farms, —
  It had the tassels on.

I thought how yellow it would look
  When Richard went to mill;
And then I wanted to get out,
  But something held my will.

I thought just how red apples wedged
  The stubble's joints between;
And carts went stooping round the fields
  To take the pumpkins in.

I wondered which would miss me least,
  And when Thanksgiving came,
If father'd multiply the plates
  To make an even sum.

And if my stocking hung too high,
  Would it blur the Christmas glee,
That not a Santa Claus could reach
  The altitude of me?

But this sort grieved myself, and so
  I thought how it would be
When just this time, some perfect year,
  Themselves should come to me.

## LVI

ON this wondrous sea,
  Sailing silently,
Knowest thou the shore
  Ho! pilot, ho!
Where no breakers roar,
  Where the storm is o'er?

In the silent west
Many sails at rest,
　　Their anchors fast;
Thither I pilot thee, —
Land, ho!  Eternity!
　　Ashore at last!

PART FIVE

The
Single Hound

One sister have I in our house,
And one a hedge away,
There's only one recorded
But both belong to me.

One came the way that I came
And wore my past year's gown,
The other as a bird her nest,
Builded our hearts among.

She did not sing as we did,
It was a different tune,
Herself to her a music
As Bumble-bee of June.

To-day is far from childhood
But up and down the hills
I held her hand the tighter,
Which shortened all the miles.

And still her hum the years among
Deceives the Butterfly,
Still in her eye the Violets lie
Mouldered this many May.

I spilt the dew but took the morn,
I chose this single star
From out the wide night's numbers,
Sue — forevermore!

*EMILY*

## I

ADVENTURE most unto itself
The Soul condemned to be;
Attended by a Single Hound —
Its own Identity.

## II

THE Soul that has a Guest,
Doth seldom go abroad,
Diviner Crowd at home
Obliterate the need,
And courtesy forbid
A Host's departure, when
Upon Himself be visiting
The Emperor of Men!

## III

$\mathcal{F}$AME is a fickle food
Upon a shifting plate,
Whose table once a Guest, but not
The second time, is set.

Whose crumbs the crows inspect,
And with ironic caw
Flap past it to the Farmer's corn;
Men eat of it and die.

## IV

$\mathcal{W}$HEN Etna basks and purrs,
Naples is more afraid
Than when she shows her Garnet
  Tooth;
Security is loud.

## V

EXHILARATION is the Breeze
That lifts us from the ground,
And leaves us in another place
Whose statement is not found;
Returns us not, but after time
We soberly descend,
A little newer for the term
Upon enchanted ground.

## VI

THE difference between despair
And fear, is like the one
Between the instant of a wreck,
And when the wreck has been.

The mind is smooth, — no motion —
Contented as the eye
Upon the forehead of a Bust,
That knows it cannot see.

## VII

THERE is a solitude of space,
A solitude of sea,
A solitude of death, but these
Society shall be,
Compared with that profounder site,
That polar privacy,
A Soul admitted to Itself:
Finite Infinity.

## VIII

THE props assist the house
Until the house is built,
And then the props withdraw —
And adequate, erect,
The house supports itself;
Ceasing to recollect
The auger and the carpenter.
Just such a retrospect

Hath the perfected life,
A past of plank and nail,
And slowness, — then the scaffolds drop —
Affirming it a soul.

IX

THE gleam of an heroic act,
Such strange illumination —
The Possible's slow fuse is lit
By the Imagination!

X

THE Soul's superior instants
Occur to Her alone,
When friend and earth's occasion
Have infinite withdrawn.

Or she, Herself, ascended
To too remote a height,
For lower recognition
Than Her Omnipotent.

This mortal abolition
Is seldom, but as fair
As Apparition — subject
To autocratic air.

Eternity's disclosure
To favorites, a few,
Of the Colossal substance
Of immortality.

## XI

*A* LITTLE madness in the Spring
Is wholesome even for the King,
But God be with the Clown,
Who ponders this tremendous scene —
This whole experiment of green,
As if it were his own!

## XII

Bloom upon the Mountain, stated,
Blameless of a name.
Efflorescence of a Sunset —
Reproduced, the same.

Seed, had I, my purple sowing
Should endow the Day,
Not a tropic of the twilight
Show itself away.

Who for tilling, to the Mountain
Come, and disappear —
Whose be Her renown, or fading,
Witness, is not here.

While I state — the solemn petals
Far as North and East,
Far as South and West expanding,
Culminate in rest.

And the Mountain to the Evening
Fit His countenance,
Indicating by no muscle
The Experience.

## XIII

THE Hills erect their purple heads,
The Rivers lean to see —
Yet Man has not, of all the throng,
A curiosity.

## XIV

IN winter, in my room,
I came upon a worm,
Pink, lank, and warm.
But as he was a worm
And worms presume,
Not quite with him at home —
Secured him by a string
To something neighboring,
And went along.

A trifle afterward
A thing occurred,
I'd not believe it if I heard —
But state with creeping blood;
A snake, with mottles rare,
Surveyed my chamber floor,
In feature as the worm before,
But ringed with power.
The very string
With which I tied him, too,
When he was mean and new,
That string was there.

I shrank — "How fair you are!"
Propitiation's claw —
"Afraid," he hissed,
"Of me?"
"No cordiality?"
He fathomed me.
Then, to a rhythm slim
Secreted in his form,
As patterns swim,
Projected him.

That time I flew,
Both eyes his way,
Lest he pursue —
Nor ever ceased to run,
Till, in a distant town,
Towns on from mine —
I sat me down;
This was a dream.

## XV

THIS quiet Dust was Gentlemen and Ladies,
      And Lads and Girls;
Was laughter and ability and sighing,
      And frocks and curls.

This passive place a Summer's nimble mansion,
      Where Bloom and Bees
Fulfilled their Oriental Circuit,
      Then ceased like these.

## XVI

$\mathcal{I}$ FIT for them,
I seek the dark till I am thorough fit.
The labor is a solemn one,
With this sufficient sweet —
That abstinence as mine produce
A purer good for them,
If I succeed, —
If not, I had
The transport of the Aim.

## XVII

𝓗ER "Last Poems" —
Poets ended,
Silver perished with her tongue,
Not on record bubbled other
Flute, or Woman, so divine;
Not unto its Summer morning
Robin uttered half the tune —
Gushed too free for the adoring,
From the Anglo-Florentine.
Late the praise —

'Tis dull conferring
On a Head too high to crown,
Diadem or Ducal showing,
Be its Grave sufficient sign.
Yet if we, no Poet's kinsman,
Suffocate with easy woe,
What and if ourself a Bridegroom,
Put Her down, in Italy?

(Written after the death of Mrs. Browning in 1861.)

## XVIII

THE Bible is an antique volume
Written by faded men,
At the suggestion of Holy Spectres —
Subjects — Bethlehem —
Eden — the ancient Homestead —
Satan — the Brigadier,
Judas — the great Defaulter,
David — the Troubadour.
Sin — a distinguished Precipice
Others must resist,
Boys that "believe"
Are very lonesome —
Other boys are "lost."
Had but the tale a warbling Teller
All the boys would come —
Orpheus' sermon captivated,
It did not condemn.

## XIX

$\mathscr{A}$ LITTLE over Jordan,
As Genesis record,
An Angel and a Wrestler
Did wrestle long and hard.

Till, morning touching mountain,
And Jacob waxing strong,
The Angel begged permission
To breakfast and return.

"Not so," quoth wily Jacob,
And girt his loins anew,
"Until thou bless me, stranger!"
The which acceded to:

Light swung the silver fleeces
Peniel hills among,
And the astonished Wrestler
Found he had worsted God!

## XX

VOLCANOES be in Sicily
And South America,
I judge from my geography.
Volcanoes nearer here,

A lava step, at any time,
Am I inclined to climb,
A crater I may contemplate,
Vesuvius at home.

## XXI

SAFE Despair it is that raves,
Agony is frugal,
Puts itself severe away
For its own perusal.

Garrisoned no Soul can be
In the front of Trouble,
Love is one, not aggregate,
Nor is Dying double.

## XXII

$\mathcal{I}$ DID not reach thee,
But my feet slip nearer every day;
Three Rivers and a Hill to cross,
One Desert and a Sea —
I shall not count the journey one
When I am telling thee.

Two deserts — but the year is cold
So that will help the sand —
One desert crossed, the second one
Will feel as cool as land.
Sahara is too little price
To pay for thy Right hand!

The sea comes last. Step merry, feet!
So short have we to go
To play together we are prone,
But we must labor now,
The last shall be the lightest load
That we have had to draw.

The Sun goes crooked — that is night —
Before he makes the bend
We must have passed the middle sea,
Almost we wish the end
Were further off — too great it seems
So near the Whole to stand.

We step like plush, we stand like snow —
The waters murmur now,
Three rivers and the hill are passed,
Two deserts and the sea!
Now Death usurps my premium
And gets the look at Thee.

# INDEX OF FIRST LINES

*Selected Poems of Emily Dickinson*

*Index of First Lines*

PAGE